BARCELONA T
GUIDE BOOK

CW00504389

Discover Barcelona in 2023, 2024 and beyond with this comprehensive guidebook, offering insights, tips, and information for an unforgettable visit.

Kian Wright

TABLE OF CONTENT

Introduction to Barcelona

2

Welcome to the vibrant city of Barcelona! Nestled along the northeastern coast of the Iberian Peninsula, this bustling metropolis is known for its rich history, stunning architecture, and dynamic cultural scene.

In this comprehensive travel guide, we'll take you on an unforgettable journey through the enchanting streets of Barcelona, sharing the must-visit attractions, hidden gems, and practical insights to make your trip truly remarkable.

From the moment you step foot in Barcelona, you'll be greeted by the juxtaposition of modernity and tradition. The city's unique architecture tells the story of its past, with influences from the Roman, Gothic, and Modernist eras. As you navigate its labyrinthine streets, you'll encounter bustling markets, tranquil squares, and vibrant neighbourhoods, each offering a different facet of Barcelona's identity.

Throughout this guide, we'll delve into the city's iconic landmarks, such as the historic districts that reveal its medieval charm, and the awe-inspiring works of Antoni Gaudi that have come to define its architectural landscape. We'll lead you to the picturesque Mediterranean beaches where you can unwind and soak up the sun, as well as introduce you to the delectable world of Catalan cuisine and tapas culture that will tantalize your taste buds.

But Barcelona isn't just about sightseeing and dining – it's a city that pulses with artistic expression, from its museums and galleries to its vibrant street art scene. We'll help you navigate the city's rich cultural offerings and showcase the local artists who shape its creative spirit.

Whether you're a sports enthusiast, a shopaholic, or a night owl, Barcelona has something to offer. From attending exhilarating football matches at Camp Nou to browsing through the trendiest boutiques and markets, and from dancing the night away in its pulsating clubs to discovering the beauty of its surrounding areas on day trips, there's no shortage of activities to keep you entertained.

In this guide, we'll also touch on practical aspects of your visit, including language tips, transportation options, and sustainable tourism initiatives that allow you to explore responsibly. By the time you reach the final chapter, you'll have gained a deep appreciation for Barcelona's diverse offerings and an understanding of what makes this city an unforgettable destination.

So, fasten your seatbelts as we embark on this journey through the captivating streets of Barcelona. Whether you're a history buff, an art lover, a foodie, or simply a traveller in search of new experiences, Barcelona promises to leave an indelible mark on your heart and memories that will last a lifetime.

How to get to Barcelona from any part of the world

Barcelona is among the top ten(10) vacation spots in Europe and has a long history of attracting business travellers. Because of this, it has excellent connections to the rest of Spain and the rest of the globe.

Departing from the U.S.

There are several non-stop flights available from different American cities to Barcelona. Some of the most popular flights are as follows:

- Chicago, Miami, New York (JFK), and Atlanta are all served by American Airlines.
- Lufthansa: Philadelphia
- Iberia: From Barcelona, "low-cost" flights are offered by the airline group IAG (Iberia, British Airways, and Aer Lingus) to several American cities, including Los Angeles and San Francisco.

Leaving from Canada

Direct flights from Canada to Barcelona are provided by these two Canadian airlines:

- Air Canada: Montreal and Toronto
- Air Transat: Five weekly direct Air Transat flights leave from Montreal.

Leaving from Australia

The following airlines provide intriguing connecting flights from different Australian locations to Barcelona:

- Emirates
- Malaysia Airlines

- Qantas
- Doha Airlines

Leaving from Europe

As Barcelona, the capital of Catalonia, draws tens of thousands of British visitors each year, several airlines provide flights from numerous British locations to this city. Every flight is direct.

- **Easyjet:** From Newcastle, Bristol, London Southend, London Gatwick, Liverpool, and Belfast.
- **Ryanair:** flies to Birmingham, Liverpool, Edinburgh, and Glasgow from London Stansted.
- **Monarch:** From Leeds Bradford, Manchester, Birmingham, London Gatwick, and.

How do I travel from the airport to the city centre?

By ferry

Visitors from the Balearic Islands can go by boat to Barcelona, which is a very alluring choice, particularly for those who wish to bring their automobile. Transmediterránea and Balearia are the two ferry companies that operate the routes.

By bus

You may get to Barcelona via bus as well. Numerous bus companies go from other Spanish towns as well as important European cities including London, Brussels, and Paris. For reference, it takes an 8-hour bus to get from Madrid to Barcelona.

By train

After Madrid's Atocha train station, Barcelona Sants train station is the busiest in all of Spain. Spain's high-speed trains (AVE) take only two and a half hours to go from Madrid to Barcelona, and they just opened a new route that travels from Paris to Barcelona in six hours.

10 Best Accommodations available near Barcelona airport

1. Hotel BAH Barcelona Airport

The tourists staying at this upscale hotel will be near Port de Barcelona and Castelldefels Beach, in the business sector, at the Barcelona Airport Hotel in El Prat de Llobregat. Wired Internet access, on-site business facilities, and free newspapers in the lobby are just a few of the hotel amenities available at El Prat de Llobregat. Additionally, 24-hour round-trip airport shuttle services are offered.

Amenities:
A free Wi-Fi hotspot, a fitness centre, a restaurant, a bar, room service, a coffee maker and a shuttle service are available.

Address: Plaça de la Volateria, 3, 08820 El Prat de Llobregat, Barcelona, Spain

2. Hotel Ibis Barcelona Fira de Cornella

The Ibis Barcelona Cornellá Hotel can be found in Cornellá de Llobregat. It is situated in the Almeda industrial area and offers quick access to both the city's downtown and Barcelona's El Prat airport. Its amenities include Wi-Fi and air-conditioned rooms, a restaurant, a bar open round-the-clock and visitor parking.

Amenities:

café, bar or lounge, Coffee shop, free parking, business centre, and free WiFi are all provided. Flat-screen TV, banquet/meeting space, Internet.

Address: Carrer Albert Einstein, 53-55, 08940 Cornellà de Llobregat, Barcelona, Spain

3. Hotel Tropical Gava Mar

The Hotel Tropical Gava Mar is the ideal choice when seeking a high-quality hotel to stay at that is near the beach and the Barcelona-El Prat airport. The nicest Barcelona beaches, which provide year-round sun and pleasure, are just outside this hotel. Located in Gava, this beachfront property is approximately a 10-minute drive from the airport and three minminutelk from Castelldefels Beach and Filipinas Beach.

Amenities:

Beachfront, Spa and Wellness Centre, Fitness Centre, Restaurant, Bar/Lounge, Room Service, Free Wi-Fi, Outdoor and Indoor Swimming Pool.

Address: Carrer dels Tellinaires, 17, 08850 Gavà, Barcelona, Spain

4. Salles Ciutat del Prat Barcelona Airport

This modern hotel is approximately an 8-minute drive from Barcelona's El Prat Airport. The Salles Ciutat del Prat Barcelona Airport has a sauna, gym, indoor pool, complimentary Wi-Fi, flat-screen TVs, and satellite TV in each room, among other amenities.

Mediterranean food is served in the on-site restaurant, the Sinfonia Restaurant. Moreover, a cafe bar serves snacks and beverages. Barcelona's Fira Congress Centre is a 15-minute drive from Ciutat del Prat. With direct access to the city centre provided by the El Prat de Llobregat train station, which is 20 minutes away by foot from the hotel, this could be the best choice for getting about the congested city centre. It might even be wiser to leave the vehicle at home. Additionally, free airport shuttles are offered every day from 4:30 to 1:30.

Amenities:

The following amenities are available: an indoor pool, a fitness centre, a restaurant, a bar or lounge, room service, a coffee shop, free WiFi and a shuttle service.

Address: Avinguda del Remolar, 46, 08820 El Prat de Llobregat, Barcelona, Spain

5. Hotel Hyatt Regency Barcelona Tower

The Hyatt Regency Barcelona Tower is situated next to the exposition centre, halfway between Barcelona's airport and the city's newest financial and corporate sector. The hotel has 280 bedrooms on 29 storeys, including a Presidential Suite, 29 suites, and 12 Duplex Suites, in addition to its stunning glass dome. There is no question that this hotel provides a high-quality stay while being accessible to Barcelona-El Prat airport.

Amenities:

Restaurant, bar/lounge, room service, free Wi-Fi, tea/coffee maker, coffee machine, business centre, indoor pool, spa and wellness centre and fitness centre.

Address: Avinguda de la Granvia de l'Hospitalet, 144, 08907 Barcelona, Spain

6. The Hesperia Fira Hotel

The Hesperia Fira Hotel in Barcelona allows visitors to take advantage of everything that the city has to offer while still enjoying the conveniences of home. spacious, comfortable rooms with a kitchen. located at a 5-minute drive from the convention centre and a mere 10-minute drive from Barcelona's El Prat airport.

Amenities:

Indoor pool, dining area, bar or lounge, free WiFi, tea or coffee maker, free toiletries, flat-screen TV.

Address: Av. Mare de Déu de Bellvitge, 3, 08907 L'Hospitalet de Llobregat, Barcelona, Spain

7. AC Hotel by Marriott Gava Mar Airport

The AC Hotel by Marriott Gava Mar Airport has 69 tastefully furnished rooms that provide a comfortable stay and makes it a fantastic place to organise conferences, meetings, and special ceremonies close to the beach. Not to mention how near it is to the airport in Barcelona-El Prat.

The hotel has an outdoor pool for guests to unwind after a long day. The Minas de Gava Archaeological Park, the Gava Museum, the botanical park, the business district, and the airport are all easily accessible by car for visitors.

Amenities:

A free Wi-Fi connection, a restaurant, a bar or lounge, a flat-screen TV, a coffee shop, room service and free toiletries are available.

Address: Carrer dels Tellinaires, 33 - 35, 08850 Gavà, Barcelona, Spain

8. Hyatt Regency Barcelona Tower

The Hyatt Regency Barcelona Tower is situated next to the exposition centre, halfway between Barcelona's airport and the city's newest financial and corporate sector. The hotel has 280 bedrooms on 29 storeys, including a Presidential Suite, 29 suites, and 12 Duplex Suites, in addition to its stunning glass dome. There is no question that this hotel provides a high-quality stay while being accessible to Barcelona-El Prat airport.

Amenities:
Restaurant, bar/lounge, room service, free Wi-Fi, tea/coffee maker, coffee machine, business centre, indoor pool, spa and wellness centre and fitness centre.

Address: Avinguda de la Granvia de l'Hospitalet, 144, 08907 Barcelona, Spain

9. Sercotel Sant Boi

If you want to be close to the Barcelona-El Prat airport as well as the Port de Barcelona and Placa d'Espanya, which are all within a 15-minute drive, a stay at Sercotel Sant Boi in Sant Boi de Llobregat (Casablanca) is practical. Additionally, this hotel is regarded as a cost-effective

lodging option in Barcelona. The hotel's amenities include a business centre, express check-in, and express check-out.

Amenities:

A fitness centre, restaurant, bar or lounge, free WiFi, coffee shop, business centre and flat-screen TV with cable or satellite service are all accessible.

Address: Ctra. de la Santa Creu de Calafell, 101, 08830 Barcelona, Spain

10. Best Western Plus Hotel Alfa Aeropuerto

A family-run hotel with reasonable rates that provides a good stay is the Best Western Plus Hotel Alfa Aeropuerto.

A peaceful and comfortable stay is provided at this hotel near Barcelona's airport.

If the situation is enjoying Barcelona while just spending one night there, its location becomes quite advantageous for individuals who are in the city for a little visit. As a result of the hotel's proximity to the Barcelona-El Prat Airport, the Cruise Pier, international exhibition centres, and trade shows.

Amenities:

Indoor pool, gym, restaurant, bar, room service, free wi-fi, tea/coffee maker, coffee maker, free airport shuttle, business centre.

Address: Carrer K Zona Franca, 08040 Barcelona, Spain

Maps and directions to explore Barcelona's top attractions and hidden gems

Here are 10 top attractions and 10 hidden gems in Barcelona, along with a brief description of what they have to offer:

Top Attractions:

1. Sagrada Família:

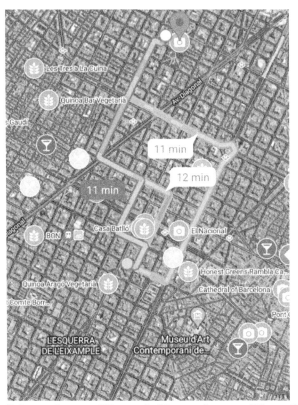

Map from Hostal Barcelona City Centre to Sagrada Família

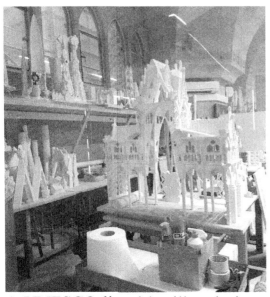

A UNESCO-listed basilica designed by Gaudí, known for its unique architecture, intricate facades, and stunning interior.

Directions: Easily accessible by metro. From Plaça Catalunya, take the L2 line to Sagrada Família station.

Contact: Address: C/ de Mallorca, 401, 08013 Barcelona, Spain

Phone: +34 932 08 04 14

2. Park Güell:

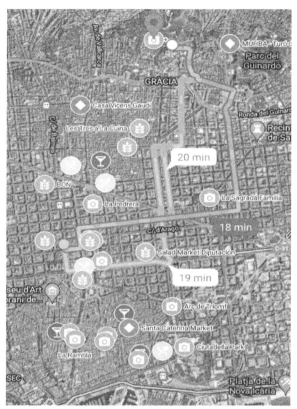

Map from Hostal Barcelona City Centre to Park Güell

A colourful public park featuring Gaudí's whimsical designs, vibrant mosaics, and panoramic views of the city.

Directions: Take the L3 metro line to Vallcarca station. From there, it's about a 15-minute walk.

Contact: Carrer d'Olot, s/n, 08024 Barcelona, Spain

Phone: +34 934 09 18 31

3. La Rambla:

Map from Hostal Barcelona City Centre to La Rambla

A bustling pedestrian street lined with shops, cafes, and street performers, perfect for people-watching and shopping.

Directions: You can walk to La Rambla from Plaça Catalunya, it's a central street in the city.

Contact: La Rambla, 08002 Barcelona, Spain

4. Casa Batlló:

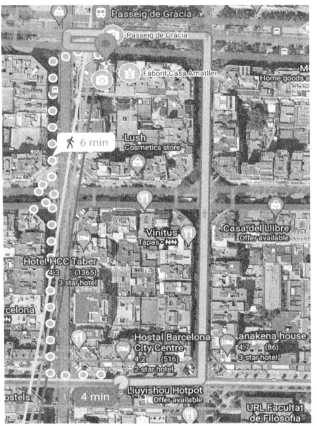

Map from Hostal Barcelona City Centre to Casa Batlló

A Gaudí-designed modernist building with a captivating facade and interior, showcasing the architect's creativity.

Directions: Situated on Passeig de Gràcia. From Plaça Catalunya, it's about a 15-minute walk.

Contact: Passeig de Gràcia, 43, 08007 Barcelona, Spain

Phone: +34 932 16 03 06
5. Camp Nou:

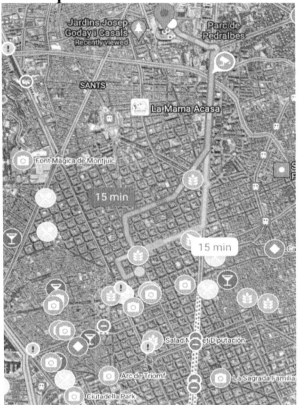

Map from Hostal Barcelona City Centre to Camp Nou

The iconic stadium of FC Barcelona offers guided tours and a chance to experience the club's history.

Directions: Take the L3 metro line to Maria Cristina station. From there, it's around a 10-minute walk.

Contact: C. d'Arístides Maillol, 12, 08028 Barcelona, Spain

Phone: +34 902 18 99 00

6. Montjuïc Hill:

Map from Hostal Barcelona City Centre to Montjuïc

A historic site with attractions like the Montjuïc Castle, Olympic Park, and stunning views over the city.

Directions: You can take the Montjuïc Funicular from Parallel metro station to the top.

Contact: Montjuïc, 08038 Barcelona, Spain

7. Barri Gòtic (Gothic Quarter):

Map from Hostal Barcelona City Centre to Barri Gòtic (Gothic Quarter)

37

A maze of narrow streets and squares filled with medieval architecture, charming shops, and cosy cafes.

Directions: Located in the city centre, easily explored on foot from Plaça Catalunya.

Contact: Barri Gòtic, 08002 Barcelona, Spain

8. Picasso Museum:

Home to an extensive collection of artworks by Pablo Picasso, showcasing his diverse styles and artistic evolution.

Directions: From Plaça Catalunya, it's about a 20-minute walk to the museum.

Contact: Carrer Montcada, 15-23, 08003 Barcelona, Spain

9. Barcelona Cathedral:

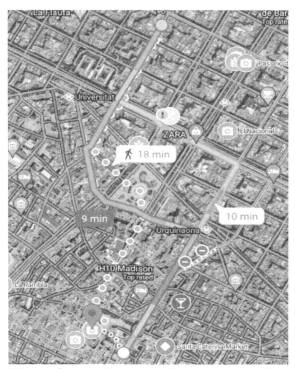

Map from Hostal Barcelona City Centre Barcelona Cathedral

A Gothic cathedral with stunning interior details and a peaceful cloister, located in the heart of the city.

Directions: Centrally located in the Gothic Quarter, a short walk from Plaça Catalunya.

Contact: Pla de la Seu, s/n, 08002 Barcelona, Spain

Phone: +34 933 15 15 54

10. Magic Fountain of Montjuïc:

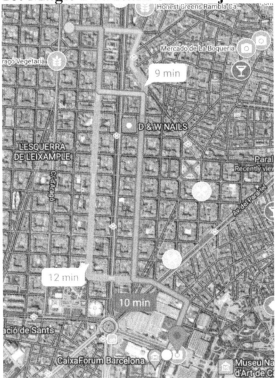

Map from Hostal Barcelona City Centre Magic Fountain of Montjuïc

A mesmerizing fountain that hosts nightly light and music shows, creating a magical atmosphere.

Directions: Take the L3 metro line to Plaça Espanya. The fountain is a short walk from there.

Contact: Plaça de Carles Buïgas, 1, 08038 Barcelona, Spain

Hidden Gems:

1. Bunkers del Carmel:

Map from Hostal Barcelona City Centre to Bunkers del Carmel

A peaceful hilltop spot offering panoramic views of the city and a perfect sunset-watching location.

Directions: Take bus 92 from Plaça Catalunya to the Bunkers del Carmel stop.

Contact: Turó de la Rovira, 08032 Barcelona, Spain

Phone: +34 932 56 21 22

2. El Born Cultural Center:

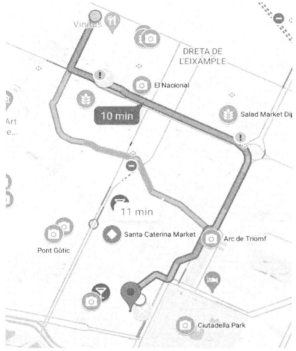

Map from Hostal Barcelona city centre to El Born Cultural Center

A unique space built over archaeological remains, providing insights into Barcelona's history and culture.
Directions: Located in El Born. From Plaça Catalunya, it's about a 20-minute walk.
Contact: Plaça Comercial, 12, 08003 Barcelona, Spain

3. Parc de Laberint d'Horta:

Map from Hostal Barcelona city centre to Parc de Laberint d'Horta

A lesser-known garden featuring a labyrinth, neoclassical statues, and serene ponds, perfect for a relaxing stroll.

Directions: Take the L3 metro line to Mundet station. The park is a 10-minute walk away.

Contact: Passeig dels Castanyers, 1, 08035 Barcelona, Spain

Phone: +34 931 53 70 10

4. Sant Pau Art Nouveau Site:

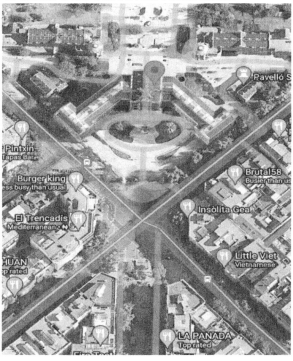

An architectural gem showcasing modernist designs and beautiful gardens, offering guided tours.

Directions: Located near Sagrada Família. From there, it's about a 15-minute walk.

Contact: Carrer de Sant Antoni Maria Claret, 167, 08025 Barcelona, Spain

Phone: +34 935 53 71 45

5. Sant Felip Neri Square:

Map from Hostal Barcelona city centre to Sant Felip Neri Square

A tranquil square with a tragic history, featuring a beautiful church and scars from the Spanish Civil War.

Directions: Located in the Gothic Quarter, a short walk from Plaça Catalunya.

Contact: Plaça de Sant Felip Neri, 08002 Barcelona, Spain

6. Palau de la Música Catalana:

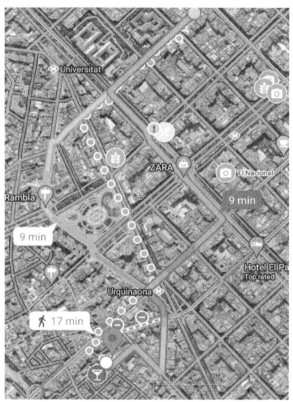

Map from Hostal Barcelona city centre to Palau de la Música Catalana

A stunning concert hall is known for its exquisite stained glass and ornate details, offering guided tours.

Directions: Centrally located. From Plaça Catalunya, it's about a 15-minute walk.

Contact: Carrer del Palau de la Música, 4-6, 08003 Barcelona, Spain

Phone: +34 932 95 72 00

7. Carrer del Bisbe:

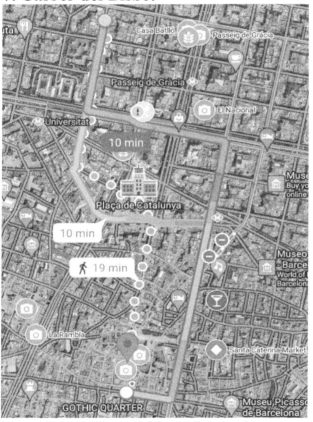

Map from Hostal Barcelona city centre to Carrer del Bisbe

A picturesque medieval street connecting the Cathedral Square to the Plaça Sant Jaume, adorned with charming details.

Directions: Located near Barcelona Cathedral in the Gothic Quarter.

Contact: Carrer del Bisbe, 08002 Barcelona, Spain

8. Mercat de la Boqueria:

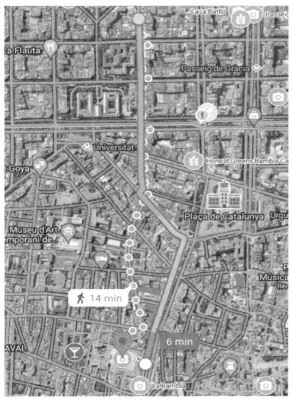

Map from Hostal Barcelona city centre to Mercat de la Boqueria

A vibrant food market filled with colourful stalls offering fresh produce, local delicacies, and more.

Directions: Located on La Rambla. Easily accessible on foot from Plaça Catalunya.

Contact: La Rambla, 91, 08001 Barcelona, Spain

9. Can Font Cultural Space:

A hidden gem showcasing traditional Catalan culture through workshops, performances, and exhibitions.

Directions: Located in Poble-sec. From Plaça Catalunya, take the L3 metro line to Poble-sec station.

Contact: Carrer del Roser, 4, 08004 Barcelona, Spain

Phone: +34 938 40 33 75

Itinerary options needed to explore Barcelona like a local

How long should I stay in Barcelona?

Barcelona stays should be for at least three to four days.

Barcelona may be seen thoroughly in 5 days without being rushed or having to forgo particular activities due to time constraints.

Barcelona is a hip city with a lively environment and plenty of young people, so you could easily spend a week there. Five days in Barcelona gives you ample time to move slowly, discover more of the city's picturesque nooks, and get a deeper understanding of the city.

Montserrat

It is advised to take a day excursion to Montserrat, the mountain and monastery, which is located approximately an hour outside of Barcelona.

Transportation in Barcelona

Barcelona has highly easy transport.

There are bus lines, a metro, and reasonably priced taxis available.

The T-10 card is often recommended for purchase on the Internet, and it does provide benefits.

The 10 tickets on the card are transferable between the bus and the metro. It will last for five travels each for a pair.

The "Barcelona Travel Card" may be purchased and offers an infinite number of travels for a certain period.

There are tickets available for two days for 16.30 euros, three days for 23.70 euros, four days for 30.80 euros, and five days for 38 euros.

A cycling tour of Barcelona

Barcelona is a highly welcoming city for cyclists. Along with the sidewalks and roadways, bicycle pathways are given special consideration. The main centre of Barcelona is flat, making cycling quite easy. There are several bicycle stands around the city, but only residents utilise them.

One of the numerous rental businesses positioned in the tourist districts offers bicycle rentals to visitors. Anyone interested in seeing all the well-known locations in Barcelona may sign up for a guided bike trip.

Barcelona Hop-on Hop-off bus

A tourist bus is the most practical method to visit the city, particularly if you are new to the area, travelling with young children or elderly people, or if you just want to be pampered and take in the view of the city from above.

The city's main tourist attractions are passed by the tourist bus, which makes stops close to each one. Any of the stations allow you to exit, explore the area on foot, and then carry on to the next location. The best part is to drive while listening to an audio tour while sitting upstairs and enjoying the view of the city.

There are three options available: the blue route, which travels past all the city's must-see attractions; the red route, which travels past additional attractions in the city; and the green route, which operates in the summer and goes by the ocean and beaches.

DAY 1

On the first day, I advise beginning with a stroll down the well-known Rambla Avenue, a lengthy pavement lined with shops selling food, flowers and trinkets. Take special care of your baggage while you're strolling as this is a busy tourist area, and be on the lookout for pickpockets.

La Rambla Avenue

La Boqueria Market is located at 91 La Rambla Street, around 20 minutes worth of walking along the La Ramblas. Fruit, vegetable, juice, chocolate, meat, spice, bakery, and other booths are available.

La Boqueria Market
Contact: Phone: +34 934 13 23 03
Address: La Rambla, 91, 08001 Barcelona, Spain
Continue strolling down the Rambla to the Gothic Quarter (Barri Gotic) after seeing the market.

Gothic Quarter

In Barcelona, the Gothic Quarter is the oldest. There, you may take a walk around the lovely lanes and many stores the area has. Even in the evening, it's pleasant to stroll there since it's lively and the stores and cafés are still open. You have the option of going on a self-guided tour or going to the Gothic Quarter.

The final station is near the promenade so that when you get there, you may spend some time strolling down the lengthy promenade that goes to the ocean and has many shops along it.

Barcelona's beach is unique in that it was upgraded and a large number of palm trees were planted there before the 1992 Summer Olympics to draw tourists. This was a very successful move, and Barcelona has since risen to the top of the list of most visited cities.

Maremagnum
Contact: Phone: +34 930 12 91 39
Address: Moll d'Espanya, 5, 08039 Barcelona, Spain
Shopping enthusiasts should be aware that the seaside region also has a mall named Maremagnum. (A short stroll of around 15 minutes).

The Aquarium and the IMAX Cinema, two attractions that are accessible on foot and well-liked by families with young children, are also nearby.

The "Diagonal Mall" is a different, more isolated mall along the coast that is home to several well-known retailers, including "Primark," a popular clothing retailer with competitive pricing.

Metro line L4 connects Selva de Mar and Barceloneta station to Barceloneta Beach and the diagonal mall. If you don't want to buy, you may relax in one of Barcelona's numerous restaurants with a drink and some tapas and simply take in the culture of the Spanish people.

DAY 2

One of the most visited tourist attractions in Barcelona is the Palau de la Msica Catalana, a music venue.

Palau de la Msica Catalana

Contact: Phone: +34 932 95 72 00

Address: C/ Palau de la Música, 4-6, 08003 Barcelona, Spain

It takes around 15 minutes to reach there on foot, by bus, or by metro. Bus routes 45, V17, and V15. L1, L4, the metro.

It was designed by architect Luis Dominic I Montaner, and it is a masterpiece. Concerts are routinely held in this edifice, which was specifically and enchanted constructed with a blend of stained glass and unique mosaics.

The fee for the visit is either 10 euros for a self-guided tour within the building or 18 euros for a tour with a guide. The price drops from 20 euros to 16 euros for reservations made 21 days in advance. Children under 10 are admitted free, while seniors pay 16 euros.

Those who bought tickets for the tour bus in the city will also get a 20% discount; the ticket must be shown at the box office. Each 30-minute interval, the tours are offered.

Daily tours of the Palau de la Musica are available from 10:00 am to 3:30 pm.

Easter and the month of July have extended hours of operation from 10:00 am to 6:00 pm. In August, the hours are extended to 9:00 am to 6:00 pm. From there, continue to Via Laietana, a prominent primary thoroughfare with striking architecture.

Via Laietana

Arc de Triomf
Contact: Phone: +34 932 85 38 34
Address: Passeig de Lluís Companys, 08003 Barcelona, Spain

Continue from there to the stunning Arc de Triomf, which was once constructed in honour of the Barcelona International Exhibition. Continue walking from the Arc de Triomf to the Parc de la Ciutadella, a citadel park close to the Arc de Triomf.

Parc de la Ciutadella
Contact: Phone: +34 638 23 71 15
Address: Passeig de Picasso, 21, 08003 Barcelona, Spain
The park, which is spectacular and lovely, was created in the middle of the 19th century. Not to be overlooked. It has a lovely lake, seating, a fountain, and the majestic Catalan Parliament building, among other things.

El Born neighbourhood

The El Born neighbourhood, also known as the La Ribera neighbourhood, is close to the Gothic Quarter, between Via Laietana and Ciutadella Park, and is one of the oldest and most picturesque parts of the city. It is accessible from this location.

There are several magnificent mediaeval palaces and structures in this region, some of which are part of the Picasso Museum complex.

A variety of vibrant restaurants, pubs, and lanes can be found in this quiet, warm, and bustling neighbourhood.

Bunkers del Carmel
Contact: Phone: +34 932 56 21 22
Address: Carrer de Marià Labèrnia, s/n, 08032 Barcelona, Spain

It is advised to get to Bunkers del Camel, Barcelona's most spectacular and chill overlook before the day ends. The greatest vantage point in Barcelona is here, offering a fantastic 360-degree view of the whole city away from the tourist crowds, on a mountain in the centre ofTomel neighbourhood next to a walking park.

To defend against bombings, fortifications were built on the 262-meter-high mountain where the Bunkers del Carmel vantage point is situated. These fortifications were built during the Spanish Civil War.

Since it is distant hardly any of the popular tourist attractions, there are hardly any visitors here.

Although the view is particularly stunnipeaceet, it is advised that those who value peace get there in the morning.

A little advice: if you still want to show up there even though an hour early and get a spot. Even though it is difficult to access, the location is entirely favoured by the locals, and around sunset, it becomes crowded.

The vantage point is a short walk from El Carmel Station, which is accessible from Plaça Catalunya by bus line 24 or the blue Metro line L5.

DAY 3

The day begins at the Jewish Mount or Montjuc. This hill is crowned by a former military stronghold. A cable car can take you up the hill in Montjuic to the fortress, from which you can enjoy a stunning view of the whole city.

If you seek directions from locals, bear in mind that the word for a cable car in Spanish is Teleférico.

Where is Montjuic located?

Take the metro to the Plaza Espaa (Plaza Espaa) station on lines L-3 or L-1 to get there.

Palau Nacional Palace
Contact: Phone: +34 936 22 03 76
Address: Palau Nacional, 08038 Barcelona, Spain
The stunning Espanya Square and the Palau Nacional Palace, which we will arrive at later, are both accessible from the metro station's exit. Currently, boards bus route 150 (his bus stop is just outside the metro).
The stronghold at the summit of Montjuic Hill is reached by Line 150 as it ascends the mountain via several stops.
One alternative is to exit the bus at the fort's entrance and go there on foot or by cable car. Another alternative is to exit the bus before reaching the fort at the Panicular station, from where the cable car departs in the direction of the fort up the hill. From there, you may exit on foot.
Price of a cable: € 13.70
Continue strolling in the direction of the Olympic Stadium after exiting the cable car in the neighbourhood.

It is Spain's sixth-largest stadium. It was built in 1929 and served as the major venue for the Olympic Games in Barcelona in 1992.

Additionally, you may stroll around the lovely parks near Montjuc:

Juan Maragall's Gardens

The Jardins de Joan Maragall, or Juan Maragall's Gardens, are only accessible at certain times.

The Palau Nacional Palace, which was constructed in 1929 for the Barcelona International Exhibition and began operating as the National Museum of Art of Catalonia in 1934, is a short walk from the Liberal Gardens and the Gardens of Juan Margal.

There is a breathtaking view of the whole city, as well as Plaza Espana, from there that must be experienced.

Espanyol Poble

Poble Espanyol
Contact: Phone: +34 935 08 63 00
Address: Av. de Francesc Ferrer i Guàrdia, 13, 08038 Barcelona, Spain

Turn left as you leave the palace, facing Plaza Espaa, and continue straight ahead to reach Pablo Espanyol. It is also worth seeing this amazing site, which is shaped like a Spanish hamlet.

Spanish-style structures separated into many zones will astonish you. There are also charming stores with craftsmen that create handmade goods like jewellery, glass, pottery, guitars, and more.

You may also have a seat at a nearby café and take in the genuine Spanish ambience. Also, be sure to see the movie about Spain's traditional festivities that are being shown somewhere.

Adult admission to Pablo Espanyol is 14 euros. (Online booking: 11.20 euros), admittance after 8 p.m.: 7, kids (4-12): 8, kids (4 and under): free, students (10.50 euros), and seniors (9 euros).

If Pueblo Espanyol is your last stop, take line 150 back to Plaza Espana to reach your starting point. (From Pueblo Espanyol's entrance, turn right to bus stop 150 which will take you back to Espanya Square and from there Metro l-3 to the hotel).

The Magic Fountains of Montjuc

The Magic Fountain of Montjuc is just next to Plaza Espana. Do not miss the fountain show if you are there during the fountain's active hours.

Every half-hour, the programme is restarted. April through May, October: Thursday through Saturday, 20:00–22:00,

June through September: Wednesday through Sunday, 21:30–22:00, and from 1 November to 31 March: Thursday through Saturday, 20:00–22:00. From January 7 to February 28, there will be no performances.

DAY 4

You should at least act like a native for one day when you visit Barcelona.

Visit the Gracia area, and there is little question that you will add to the experiences already in your bag. For those who are interested, there is a guided trip that includes admission to all three of Gaudi's stunning structures.

Villa de Garcia

The Gracia district, which includes the well-known neighbourhoods of Villa de Garcia and Garcia Nova, is the oldest and most genuine district in Barcelona.

Until the end of the 17th century, the Garcia area was a distinct community from the sprawling city of Barcelona; yet, it continues to operate as a separate province.

The route leading to the village was Passeig de Gràcia. The Festa Major de Gràcia, which takes place every year in August and is celebrated across the neighbourhood, is the event that gives the area its most well-known reputation.

The neighbourhood is home to many young families, students, and artists. It also includes a variety of pubs, stores, galleries, and fine cafés, as well as several entertainment venues. The area is home to several lovely squares, a large number of eateries, and a charming tiny market called Libertat.

Placa de la Virreina

Plaça de La Vila de Gràcia

Placa del Sol

Cafe del Sol
Address: Plaça del Sol, 16, 08012 Barcelona, Spain
Phone: +34 932 37 14 48
The neighbourhood's three major squares are Placa de la Virreina, which is centred around an ancient church, Plaça de La Vila de Gràcia, and Placa del Sol, where Cafe del Sol is located and is regarded as the neighbourhood's oldest café.

Casa Vicens

Contact: Phone: +34 932 71 10 64

Address: Carrer de les Carolines, 20-26, 08012 Barcelona, Spain

Casa Vicens, the first structure Gaudi created in the region between 1883 and 1878 for the ceramics maker Manuel Vicens, is another fascinating location.

What you should know about Gràcia is that it is a lovely area that is suggested for trips as well as for particular shopping, relaxing in cafes, and learning about the nightlife.

The Gracia neighbourhood is the place to go for people who are interested in spending a few days in the heart of Barcelona's tourism, getting away from the tourist districts, and experiencing a unique environment.

For those who like shopping, there are discount speciality shops, big malls and lesser-known businesses here.

Park Guell

Contact: Phone: +34 934 09 18 31

Address: 08024 Barcelona, Spain

You may explore Park Guell, a garden complex created by famed architect Antonio Gaudi, after taking a walk around Gracia.

In 2005, UNESCO named the location a World Heritage Site.

On your way to Park Guell

Without question, Gaudi's Park Guell is one of Barcelona's most well-known structures. Osby Goel hired him because he wanted to design a chic park for the Barcelona elite.

There are several entrances to the park.

The main entry from Carrer d'Olot is the most magnificent. There are two pavilions there, one of which is a small museum, and at the top of the steps is the well-known dragon monument. The park-like granite pillars that seem to emerge from the earth-like tree trunks have a lot to offer.

Gaudi was profoundly inspired by and incorporated natural shapes into his artwork.

A beautiful view of the whole park and Barcelona may be found at the summit of the park. The park also has a small eatery where you can get something to eat and some sangria.

How can I access the park?

Bus route 24 may take passengers to the park. The bus stop for it is close to Plaça Catalunya. It takes 30 minutes to get here.

You'll be dropped off at Park Guell's entrance by Line 24. There are two areas in the park: one is free and the other costs 10 euros for adults. You may climb the steps within the park to get a wonderful perspective of the city.

You should be aware that there are lengthy lines and a limited amount of tickets for the paid section. Thus, it is advised to get tickets in early!

This a valuable tip to be aware of!

The paid section is free before and after the set opening times (6–8 in the morning and 9–11 at night).

Sagrada Familia

Contact: Phone: +34 932 08 04 14

Address: C/ de Mallorca, 401, 08013 Barcelona, Spain

You will go to the Sagrada Familia after the visit to Park Guell. the most well-known church Gaudi built in Barcelona. Its construction started in 1883 and is still in its early stages today. 2026 is the projected completion date.

How do I go from Park Güell to Sagrada Familia?

Exit by the same gate you came in at Park Güell. (If you are already in the low portion of the park at the second gate, proceed up the steps and continue straight until you reach the entry gate).

The bus that travels to Sagrada Familia stops at the v-19 station, which is a few metres straight after turning right at the gate. Leave the train station.

Pg. de Sant Joan-Rosselló and it takes 10 minutes to walk there to get to the Sagrada Familia.

Be careful to see the Sagrada Familia from all sides since she has two sides, each of which has a distinct appearance. It makes sense that the Sagrada Familia is the most visited tourist attraction in Barcelona.

Only after taking a stroll around the church can you appreciate the abundance of decorations and sculptures that line its exterior.

The church's main hall is extremely magnificent, so you shouldn't skip taking a quick walk inside. It is also feasible and advised to pay a charge to enter to be astounded by the unusual construction within.

Continue using the metro until you arrive at Diagonal station, where you exit for Passeig de Gracia.

Casa Mila

Casa Mila
Contact: Phone: +34 932 14 25 76
Address: Pg. de Gràcia, 92, 08008 Barcelona, Spain

Reach Casa Mila, also known as La Federer, an apartment complex designed by Gaudi between 1905 and 1910, by turning left onto Carrer de Provenca. You may take a tour of the structure, go inside one of the apartments, and explore the little Gaudi-themed museum in the attic. The top of the structure, which has quirky-shaped chimneys, vibrant mosaics, and a stunning perspective of the city, is unquestionably the highlight of the tour.

Casa Mila is located at 261-265 Carrer de Provença and is open from 9:00 to 20:00.

Batllo House

Retrace your steps to the fashionable Passeig de Gracia, where you may see the shops, cafés, and restaurants.

It's hard to go by the 43rd building on the block without pausing to appreciate it.

The 1906 Casa Batlló, which Gaudi both constructed and planned, is notable for its corrugated windows, curving balconies, blue, green, and purple porcelain inlaid walls, and wavy, blue-tiled roof.

The roof, which is shaped like a dragon, is meant to represent St. George, who, by Christian tradition, slayed the dragon. You should go inside and have a look around the structure, which is filled with circular, colourful, and vegetarian features that may make you a little dizzy.

DAY 5

It is advised to do one of the well-liked day excursions from Barcelona after four excellent days there.

Montserrat

A day excursion to Montserrat is the most well-known and stunning of them. The highlight of this journey for many tourists is a trip to the Monastery of Montserrat in Barcelona, Spain, which is located in the Catalonia area. Some people think that Montserrat also means the Sacred Mount of Teeth, and when you see the location you will quickly understand why.

About an hour by rail northwest of Barcelona, there is a Benedictine monastery called Montserrat that is built into a stunning mountain.

The monastery not only has a long history and is of great religious significance, but the breathtaking vistas that surround it are now enough of a cause to make a trip.

If you enjoy walking, some particularly interesting trails pass through the mountains surrounding the monastery, where you can experience stunning views of the distinctive stone textures that exist throughout Catalonia. However, it is also a national park that includes a jagged and unusual mountain range, so it is not just this monastery.

With the aid of the local cable car and funicular, you can also climb to the mountain's summit. From there, you may choose from several various hiking paths that all circle the spectacular views of the rural Catalonia area, which are quite different from Barcelona's urban landscape.

What Can You Do in Montserrat?

The monastery is the area's most well-known landmark, drawing a large number of pilgrims. The site's main structure, a dark and elaborate 16th-century basilica, the church, is open to visitors but guests are not permitted inside the monastery. The sanctuary of the location is the Black Madonna statue, which is located in a little niche above the main altar.

Plaça de Santa Mara

You may also visit the Plaça de Santa Mara, a square in front of the monastery, and the Museu de Montserrat, which showcases contemporary artwork created by Spanish painters including Dali and Picasso. Sardana dances, the national dance of Catalonia, are performed in the church plaza on Sunday afternoons and sometimes even later.

The hikers will choose to follow the tougher and longer routes at the summit, but two more routes may be completed in the monastery region with an easy walk of 3 km. This is not a terrible choice for those who don't go well.

Ridge of Montserrat:

In addition to viewing the chapel, you may go trekking in the nearby mountains since the whole of Monster's Ridge is a natural reserve. providing distinctive landscapes, opportunities for observation, living things, and cliffs for mountain climbers.

Among other things, you may see from the Pyrenees routes and even see Ibiza and Majorca in the distance.

It is advised to stay up to date with the Mansrat or Plaça Catalunya tourist offices for information on the many routes and possibilities in the region.

If you are unsatisfied with the monastery and decide to take the funicular up to Sant Joan station, the area offers at least three routes that you can take (walk to a high observation point, walk to the monastery's "cave," and the route to Path of La Font Seca and Path of Les Batteries, all of which are divided into varying degrees of difficulty).

Anyone who wishes to escape the bustling metropolis and explore the natural beauty nearby can take a day excursion from Barcelona.

Tips needed for your 5 days itinerary in Barcelona

1. Travel insurance is necessary.

T rip insurance can safeguard you and your belongings, guarantee a tranquil trip, and save many heartaches. For all kinds of excursions and holidays in Europe and throughout the globe, it is advised to spend a relatively minimal amount on insurance.

2. Don't Hire A Vehicle

Travel toot Barcelona, you do not need to hire a vehicle. In addition to two tour bus lines that will transport you to all the main attractions, the city has a reliable underground system with stations dispersed throughout it, and you can also get about on foot.

You may visit the same sights and take in the ambience without leaving the busy tourist regions.

3. Watch Out For Pickpockets

Like every other big, touristic city in the globe, Barcelona has a reputation for being a location where pickpockets are common. Use a money belt to protect yourself against pickpockets and disperse the danger among your bag, luggage, pockets, and other personal belongings. You should always store your belongings safely in busy areas, wherever you are in the globe.

4. Map and orientation

The city is quite simple to navigate, particularly because all the important locations are marked with signage. In addition, Google Maps functions flawlessly offline. You can download an offline Barcelona map and use it without an internet connection. In addition, there is WiFi available in many cafes and stores, as well as the Barcelona WiFi network, which you can access for free throughout the city if you enter your email address.

5. Leave Barcelona For A Day Trip
Utilise your time in Barcelona to go on a day excursion. Figueres and Girona are both within a two-hour drive, or you may go to the renowned Montserrat Monastery.

Accommodation options suitable for 5 days itinerary

In this regard, I will be recommending about 2 accommodation options which are Hotels and Hostels

The three best hotels in Barcelona
There are a tonne of places to stay in Barcelona if you're not interested in staying in a hostel, but these are my personal favourites:

1. Room Mate Pau Hotel

99

It's a trendy and contemporary hotel located near Diagonal Metro Station in the Eixample neighbourhood. With the use of unique lighting features, the design is simple and uses light colours. LCD TVs and Wi-Fi are both provided in the rooms.

Address: C/ de Fontanella, 7, 08010 Barcelona, Spain

2. Hotel Ohla Bracelona

A stunning location, a 5-star boutique hotel that is ideal for couples. The hotel's roof has a unique bar, and in the evenings, locals frequent it, creating a fantastic ambience. The rooms are well-designed. The hotel is in a great position.

You better be very nice with whoever you travel with since the rooms are unusual in that the shower is directly in the centre of the room and the toilet is in a hidden cubby in the wall.

Address: Via Laietana, 49, 08003 Barcelona, Spain

3. Hotel Casal Camper

A stylish and vibrant hotel in the Ravel neighbourhood, near La Rambla. The minimalistic interior design of the rooms makes them seem roomy and cosy. Along with the standard fixtures, they also feature wonderfully cosy couches and a hammock that hangs from the ceiling.

Sandwiches, salads, fruit, desserts, and other snacks are available 24 hours a day in the minibar. A gym, billiards bar and patio with city views are also included.

Address: Carrer d'Elisabets, 11, 08001 Barcelona, Spain

Barcelona's Best Hostels

1. Party Hostel Kabul

The best venue in Barcelona to socialise and have a good time is rather than a doubt here!
The bathrooms, showers, and rooms are communal, but if you're in the city to party and meet other travellers, this is a

terrific location to stay. The hostel, which is close to La Rambla and situated in the Gothic Quarter, provides its visitors with free city excursions, pub and club tours, as well as a variety of events including barbeque nights and drinking contests. There is also a pleasant roof patio in addition to the standard amenities found in every hostel, like a common kitchen, laundry facilities, and free Wi-Fi at the computer stations.

Address: Pl. Reial, 17, 08002 Barcelona, Spain

2. Yeah Hostel

Awe-inspiring hostel, for sure! There are many things to do, pleasant staff, evening meals so you can meet people, and the walking tours are great. You can go about it rather easily because of how near it is to the metro. Really pleasant and tidy rooms are also available. After supper, they go on a pub crawl. A lot of the tourist attractions are conveniently close by, which is fantastic, and many of the renowned Barcelona neighbourhoods you wish to see are within walking distance.

Address: C/ de Girona, 176, 08037 Barcelona, Spain

3. The Central House Barcelona Gracia (Radamon Hostel)

Technological nomads' hostel. Very well-maintained hostel with a sizable deck. The majority of the guests who are here throughout the day work on computers, thus this is not a place to socialise or rejoice. This is not a party hostel. This location is ideal if you're searching for a peaceful, high-quality place to work from.

Address: C/ de Còrsega, 302, 08008 Barcelona, Spain

Museums and Galleries in Barcelona

Barcelona's top museums are among the greatest in all of Europe. Why wouldn't they be? The capital city of Catalonia is home to some of the world's finest works of art, and the city's museums and galleries honour the many creative geniuses that came from this region.

You can discover everything, including cubism, impressionism, modernism, and post-modernism.

One of the nicest things to do in Barcelona is to wander from one art treasure trove to another, particularly if you can end the day at a rooftop bar to reflect on all the enchantment you've consumed. With famous permanent exhibits and a never-ending stream of temporary ones that are deserving of all the praise in the world, Barcelona's museums are one giant love letter to art.

1. Fundació Antoni Tàpies

In 1984, Catalan artist Antoni Tàpies established this location for the research and enjoyment of modern art. Today, it serves as a museum and cultural institution devoted to Tàpies's work and life. Admire the building's tangled crown of metal netting and aluminium pipes from the outside, and inside, see Tàpies's artwork. In the 1950s, Tàpies was known for using trash, muck and rags in his paintings. Later, he progressed to include things like full pieces of furniture and flowing water.

Contact: Phone: +34 934 87 03 15

Address: C/ d'Aragó, 255, 08007 Barcelona, Spain

2. Picasso Museum de Barcelona

Nearly 4,000 works make up the permanent collection, most of which depict young Pablo's formative years at art school and his subsequent interactions with Catalonia's fin-de-siècle avant-garde. the gallery of mature Cubist paintings, the creative temporary exhibits, and the unparalleled continuous display of the artist's progress from teenage portraiture to the dramatic innovations of his Blue Period.

Visit at lunchtime or just before the last admittance to avoid punishingly large lines, or purchase your tickets online in advance.

Contact: Phone: +34 932 56 30 00

Address: C/ de Montcada, 15-23, 08003 Barcelona, Spain

3. Museu Nacional d'Art de Catalunya

The Catalan National Art Museum offers a fantastic overview of Catalan art from the 12th to the 20th century. For the magnificent Gothic collection, the fascinating Romanesque collection, and the distinctively Catalan modernista collection. Additionally, you have earned that breathtaking perspective of the city below after you have ascended the stairs to the old castle.

Arrive in Gresca if looking for a quiet evening activity. This quaint pub, which is close to the museum, offers a reasonable cuisine as well as a wide variety of natural wines.

Contact: Phone: +34 936 22 03 60

Address: Palau Nacional, Parc de Montjuïc, s/n, 08038 Barcelona, Spain

4. Centre de Cultura Contemporània de Barcelona

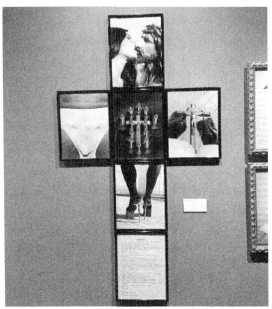

The Barcelona Centre of Contemporary Culture is located in a former almshouse that was constructed on the grounds of a mediaeval monastery. Its three rooms are host to constantly changing exhibits with a focus on multimedia arts. A regular schedule of interviews and guest speakers, including well-known figures from across the world discussing vital modern themes, may be found on the calendar. The fifth-floor viewpoint, which offers breathtaking views of the mountains, city, and sea, is open for free on the first Sunday of every month.

Contact: Phone: +34 933 06 41 00

Address: C/ de Montalegre, 5, 08001 Barcelona, Spain

5. CaixaForum Barcelona

There are three spectacular halls for temporary exhibits, which are often among the most fascinating displays to be found in the city, in addition to the permanent collection of modern art. Once inside, you may tour the pathways and spectacular terraces of the structure, a rebuilt century-old yarn and textile mill that is a marvel of industrial Catalan modernism with views of course.

Contact: Phone: +34 934 76 86 00

Address: Av. de Francesc Ferrer I Guàrdia, 6-8, 08038 Barcelona, Spain

6. Arts Santa Mònica

A new museum has opened up shop on La Rambla, welcoming practically all forms of art and endeavour but placing a particular emphasis on Catalan digital media. Everything from architecture to the performing and visual arts to music, literature, design, cuisine, and more are included in the exhibitions and events that are offered.

Contact: Phone: +34 935 67 11 10
Address: La Rambla, 7, 08002 Barcelona, Spain
7. Can Framis Museum

A cultural centre with over 300 pieces on show that were created during the last 50 years by both well-known and little-known Catalan sculptors, painters, and photographers. The structure itself, a striking renovation that highlights the building's historical elements while introducing a new element of sharp angles and poured concrete, is perhaps the star of the show. Sunlight streams through plate glass to illuminate the exhibits in a delightfully natural manner.

Contact: Phone: +34 933 20 87 36

Address: Carrer de Roc Boronat, 116, 126, 08018 Barcelona, Spain

8. Barcelona museum of contemporary art

A significant improvement in the Raval neighbourhood's fortunes was marked by Richard Meier's imposing white behemoth of a museum, which continues to stand as a beacon of modernity both outside and within. While its permanent holdings mostly include Catalan and Spanish artists, its temporary exhibits have a wider global emphasis. It holds the city's largest collection of modern art, which in this context denotes "post World War I." A helpful hint is to keep an eye out for the skateboarders who have adopted the plaza in front as their second home.

Contact: Phone: +34 934 12 08 10

Address: Plaça dels Àngels, 1, 08001 Barcelona, Spain

9. Virreina Palace

You may participate in events and exhibits relating to photography and the image, whether it be still or moving, silent or with audio, at this hub for visual production. You won't pay a dime to enter and take in the architecture or the artworks since they are all housed in a former Baroque palace smack in the centre of La Rambla.

Contact: Phone: +34 933 16 10 00

Address: La Rambla, 99, 08002 Barcelona, Spain

10. Joan Miró Foundation

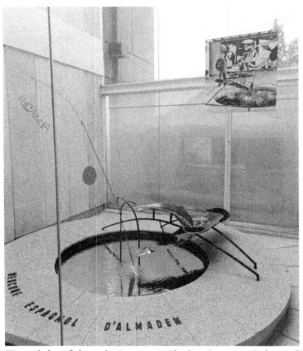

For his friend Joan Miró, Josep Llus Sert created one of the most magnificent museum structures in the world, which exquisitely fuses art and architecture and holds a vast art collection, including all of Miró's graphic works. The outdoor sculpture exhibition is a feast for the senses in and of itself, with the added pleasure of being surrounded by the natural beauty of Parc de Montjuc, in addition to the permanent collection showcasing Miró's signature use of primary colours and basic organic shapes.

Contact: Phone: +34 934 43 94 70

Address: Parc de Montjuïc, s/n, 08038 Barcelona, Spain

Festivals and Events in Barcelona

Barcelona is a city with vibrant and lively festivals that celebrate its culture all year long. Here, you can visit hopping bars and nightclubs, or travel all over the city checking out traditional street parties. You can see famed music festivals, celebrations of community and subculture and wild parties dedicated to saints.

You'll find dozens of these festivals held all year long, all over the city. Check out the 13 best festivals in Barcelona to celebrate art, culture and life with parties all year long and make your holiday one to remember.

1. The Sónar Festival

One of the biggest and most renowned experimental electronica events in the world, Sónar offers what may be the greatest party you've ever experienced. The festival, which takes place every June, attracts both well-known performers and undiscovered up-and-comers. The whole festival week is highlighted by street and club parties around the city, as well as 'unofficial' mashups and other absurd events that only serve to accentuate the music being played.

The festival emphasises multimedia art and design in addition to music as its main attraction. You may see breathtaking light displays, video performances, and other performing arts. Only 15 minutes east of the city core lies Advanced Music S.L., which serves as the main venue.

2. Música als Parcs

Free performances of jazz and classical music are presented across the city as part of the Msica als Parcs festival. The festival, which runs from June to August, started in the early 2000s and is still going strong today. Top local, emerging, and international jazz and classical performers may be seen during the concert series, which takes place outdoors in public parks. At this event, you may unwind to upbeat classical stylings or chill jazz rhythm and blues while taking in these lovely landscapes.

If you want to come, check the schedule to see if there have been any changes because of bad weather. Make sure to arrive early and get a decent seat for the performance since the concerts may become packed.

3. Holi Festival of Colours

Festival of Colours Holi Spain's version of the well-known Hindu festival is in Barcelona. The event celebrates the entrance of spring and is filled with lively entertainment and joyful activities. Participants splash each other with vibrant colours while dancing around Barcelona's streets. It's a joyful day to celebrate the end of winter and the victory of good over evil.

The thrilling paint-throwing activities are complemented by food trucks and live music. Each hue stands for a certain symbol, such as beauty, love, harvest, or fresh beginnings. DJs play pounding electronic music for the vast throng while they clean their faces of powder and paint.

4. Sala Montjuïc outdoor film festival

Live jazz performances are presented at the Sala Montjuc outdoor film festival on the lawn and in the open air. It's a good idea to arrive early or purchase tickets in advance for this event, which is held every Monday, Wednesday, and Friday, to get a decent place before the throng. A bar and takeout food stands are available, or you may bring your picnic supplies if you're seeking to get some food and beverages.

The Montjuc fortress's grounds, which rise magnificently beyond the screen, are where the event is hosted. The location is around 20 minutes south of the city's downtown. Barcelona, Spain's Ctra. de Montjuc, 66, 08038

5. Castellers de Barcelona

A Catalan custom known as Castellers de Barcelona involves the construction of very tall human towers. The first Barcelona club was established in 1969, although the custom had its origins in the rural town of Valls in the 18th century. Castellers are classic festival performers, and seeing them climb and stack to create their human towers is an adrenaline-pumping show. Nowadays, throughout their season from June to November, Castellers often provide crowd entertainment.

The skill of castle construction takes a lot of practice for Castellers to perfect. A little child climbs the 'castle' after building the foundation and vertical columns. They gesture to the audience as they ascend to mark the castle's coronation.

Barcelona, Spain is where Carrer de Bilbao, 212-214, is located.

Open Tuesday through Thursday from 7 p.m. to 9 p.m. and Friday from 7 p.m. to 11 p.m. (Monday through Wednesday, Saturday, and Sunday are closed)

Phone: +34 934 98 27 28

6. Guitar BCN festival

The Guitar BCN Festival is a pleasant occasion that features performances by a variety of musicians in the classical, jazz, or rock genres. This festival draws thousands of visitors to Barcelona and is held in several locations across the city. This festival, which has been running for more than 25 years and is sponsored by The Project in the city centre, features performances by renowned national and international performers. Past performances have included David Byrne, Pat Metheny, Vincente Amigo, and John Williams.

Whether you like jazz, blues, rock, or flamenco, there is a Guitar Festival performance that will appeal to you. You have a wide window of opportunity to attend the event, which spans from late winter to mid-summer.

Location: Barcelona, Spain (Avinguda Diagonal, 482, 08006)

7. Barcelona Eat Street Festival

The fascinating food festival Eat Street offers a diverse takeover of the streets by food trucks serving both local and foreign fare, appealing to the gourmet in you. You will undoubtedly find something to pique your hunger here, regardless of the kind of cuisine you prefer. You may also discover alternatives for vegetarian, gluten-free, and other special diets. The event is free to enter, although the prices of the food trucks vary.

Even so, the cost of a main course is reasonable here. Drinks are often not provided by food sellers; instead, a separate drink booth sells them. The event, which welcomes dogs, takes place each month along Plaça de Margarida Xirgu in the heart of the city.

Barcelona, Spain 08004 Plaça de Margarida Xirgu Poble-sec

8. Barcelona's Pride festival

Every year, the Pride event in Barcelona is a colourful and exuberant celebration of the LGBTQ community's freedom, acceptance, respect, and variety. Pride aims to provide something for everyone, despite its emphasis on this group, so that people may stand side by side and celebrate our uniqueness, love, and life. To spread its message across the city, the festival, which features a march along the streets, food booths, live music, and entertainment, collaborates with neighbourhood businesses.

The festival serves to educate as well as amuse since each year's topics range from personal choice to HIV awareness and many more. Every year in June, the Festival takes place in the Eixample District.

9. Fiestas con Correfocs del Barrio de Gràcia

The hottest block party of the year in the Gràcia neighbourhood is Fiestas with Correfocs del Barrio de Gràcia. Thousands of people gather in the lively squares of Gràcia to decorate the area with creative decorations. All ages are present at street events including dancing, card games, and outdoor music. On the vibrantly coloured streets, everyone has fun and appreciates one another's company.

The seven-day festival is filled with enjoyable events that bring people from all walks of life together. While strolling each adorned street, see parades, foam parties, live music performances, and fire runs. The festival's schedule also includes traditional music, dancing lessons, and wine tastings. During the celebrations, don't forget to cast your vote for the street and square you like.

10. Festival Cruïlla

A diverse group of musicians from all around the globe are featured at the exciting Cruilla Festival. The only need for entry into this music festival is that the musicians produce excellent music, which distinguishes it from others. Each year in July, the event has included hundreds of artists, including Gogol Bordello, Cat Power, Robert Plant, and Iggy Pop.

The Parc del Forum serves as the primary venue for the festival, where you can watch both established musicians and your favourite big-name performances. From the city core, it takes about 20 minutes to go along the coast to the Parc del Forum.

Location: C. de Pujades, 77, 2n, 7a, 08005 Barcelona, Spain

Phone: +34 937 07 33 43

Culinary Delights to Taste in Barcelona

Here's a list of popular dishes and where you can find them:
Tapas:

Try a variety of small dishes like patatas bravas, jamón ibérico, and Spanish omelette. Visit "El Xampanyet" at Carrer de Montcada, 22, 08003 Barcelona.
Paella:

A must-try dish, often featuring saffron-infused rice with seafood or meat. Head to "Can Solé" at Carrer de Sant Carles, 4, 08003 Barcelona for a great paella.

Crema Catalana:

This is a delicious dessert similar to crème brûlée. Enjoy it at "Els Quatre Gats" on Carrer de Montsió, 3, 08002 Barcelona.

Churros with Chocolate:

Savour crispy churros dipped in rich, thick chocolate sauce. Visit "Granja La Pallaresa" at Carrer de Petritxol, 11, 08002 Barcelona.

Seafood at La Boqueria Market:

Explore the vibrant La Boqueria Market for fresh seafood. It's located at La Rambla, 91, 08001 Barcelona.

Cava:

Don't miss out on tasting Spanish sparkling wine. Visit "Cava Codorníu" at Avinguda de Jaume Codorníu, s/n, 08770 Sant Sadurní d'Anoia, Barcelona.

Calçots:

If you're visiting during the calçot season (January to April), try these sweet grilled spring onions with romesco sauce. Look for local restaurants offering calçotada events.

Pintxos in Poble Sec:

Enjoy Basque-style tapas on toothpicks. Check out "La Tieta" at Carrer de Blai, 17, 08004 Barcelona.

Fideuà:

A seafood dish similar to paella but made with thin noodles. Taste it at "Elche" on Carrer de la Riereta, 5, 08001 Barcelona.

Esqueixada:

This is a refreshing Catalan salad made with salted cod, tomatoes, onions, and olive oil. Find it at various local restaurants.

Enjoy your culinary journey in Barcelona!

Barcelona nightlife and activities

Nightclubs in Barcelona are some of the best attractions the city has to offer. After dusk, the town offers a wide range of activities that last into the early hours of the morning.

If you're interested in the club scene, Barcelona's local nightlife has a lot to offer, whether you like music, drinks, ambience, or a mix of all the most crucial qualities.

Here are some best 5 to visit

1. Moog

The well-known nightclub in town, Moog, offers two levels of entertainment in a structure that has served as a location for events for more than a century. It's ideally situated in the centre of Barcelona, so it's neseveralber of other well-known sites.

There are two levels of fun at this club, but each one offers a different experience. You'll discover the mirror room, which has more pop-oriented shows, on the upper level. House and underground techno are being played in the meanwhile on the ground level.

Address:: Barcelona, Spain, Carrer de l'Arc del Teatre, 3, 08002

Time: Opening From 9.30 p.m. until 3.30 a.m. every day

Phone: +34 933 19 17 89

2. Pacha Barcelona

A famous nightclub in the city, Pacha Barcelona often has a different musical genre every day, making repeated trips exciting and novel. Here, local, national, and international DJs often perform, so you may get a wonderful mix of talent providing the background music for a night to remember.

This club's interior design is renowned for its Ibiza-inspired spherical forms and red and white-colour scheme.

It is situated between Platja del Somorrostro and Casino Barcelona, which makes it one of the greatest locations in the city.

Address: Barcelona, Spain's 08005 Carrer de Ramon Trias Fargas,

Time: Wednesday through Friday, 5 p.m.–1 a.m.; Saturday and Sunday, noon–1 a.m. (Closed: Monday– Tuesday)

Phone: +34 647 83 57 51

3. Disco City Hall

For those interested in techno and house music with a disco feel, residents and tourists alike frequent Disco City

Hall. Most of the DJs that perform here are local artists who excel at mingling with the audience.

If you want a more luxurious experience when you go, think about reserving one of the VIP tables, which has plenty of bottles for you and your guests to enjoy. This club is located close to Plaça de Catalunya in the northwest.

Address: Barcelona, Spain (Rambla de Catalunya, 2, 4, 08007)

Phone: +34 660 76 98 65

4. Sala Apolo

For many years, Sala Apolo has served as a music venue. Throughout the week, themed club nights are held there. On Monday and Tuesday evenings, for instance, indie rock will predominate, but other nights, like Wednesday, may have a wide variety of genres.

You should arrive at this nightclub before 1 am if you want to go. They usually stop allowing people in at that point since they are at capacity. This club can be reached on foot from Parallel Station and is located next to Teatre Victoria.

Address: Barcelona, Spain, Carrer Nou de la Rambla, 113, 08004

Phone: +34 934 41 40 01

5. Input

Input is an expensive dance hall that features superior sound and presents musical and dance innovation and experimentation. As a result, you may take advantage of everything that club culture has to offer throughout your vacation.

When you enter this club, you'll see that the walls are built to amplify the music in a manner that immerses the audience as much as possible while maintaining a stylish industrial aesthetic. This club may be found a short distance southwest of Font Màgica de Montjuc.

Address: 13 Av. Francesc Ferrer I Guàrdia, 08038 Barcelona, Spain

Sports and Recreation activities in Barcelona

On the country's coast, the bustling city of Barcelona can be found. This travel guide was also created to assist you in getting the most out of your water sports and leisure activities in this stunning location. Barcelona offers everything, from exhilarating activities to tranquil coastal pleasures. Let's start now!

For ease of exploration, we'll cut this schedule down to five days.

Arrival and beach exploration on Day 1

Morning: Arrive at Barcelona-El Prat Airport in the morning, then check into your lodging. Every kind of traveller may find a hotel or apartment in the city. Hotel Arts Barcelona, W Barcelona, and H10 Marina Barcelona and also there are other ones listed in the previous chapter.

Afternoon: Visit one of the city's most well-liked beaches, Barceloneta Beach. Take a leisurely walk along the sandy beaches, bask in the sunshine, and enjoy the mesmerising views of the Mediterranean Sea. At a seaside restaurant like Can Paixano or La CovaFundaa, don't forget to sample some delectable fish.

Barceloneta Beach.

Evening: Take a stroll around the thriving Port Vell district, which is close to the beach. Visit the renowned Maremagnum retail complex, which has a wide selection of eateries, stores, and entertainment venues. Enjoy a delicious meal at El Xiringuito Escribà, a restaurant renowned for its excellent seafood and breathtaking views of the coastline.

Maremagnum retail complex
Contact: Phone: +34 930 12 91 39
Address: Moll d'Espanya, 5, 08039 Barcelona, Spain
Adventures in Scuba Diving and Snorkelling on Day 2
Morning: Early in the morning, go on an exhilarating scuba diving trip. Numerous diving shops in Barcelona provide guided dives for both novice and expert divers. Dive into the Mediterranean Sea's crystal-clear waters to discover the underwater landscape alive with vibrant marine life. Blue Water Diving and Barcelona Diving Centre are two prominent dive shops.

Barcelona Diving Centre
Contact: Phone: +34 670 51 42 15
Address: Av. del Litoral, 86, 96, 08005 Barcelona, Spain
Afternoon: After your dive, continue your underwater exploration by snorkelling. Visit the lovely bay of Cala Morisca, nearby, which has clear waters ideal for snorkelling. As you swim through schools Of fish and uncover secret treasures below the surface, take in the beautiful marine ecology.

Cala Morisca

Address: Ctra. de Rat Penat a, Avinguda de Plana Novella, Km. 3.5, 08870 Sitges, Barcelona, Spain

Evening: Return to the city and treat yourself to a delicious supper at the famed seafood restaurant La Gavina, which is renowned for its superb Catalan cuisine. Enjoy delicious fresh seafood dishes while taking in expansive city views.

La Gavina Restaurant

La Gavina Restaurant

Contact: Phone: Passeig de la Ribera, 5, 08870 Sitges, Barcelona, Spain

Address: +34 938 94 15 84

Experience with Sailing and Windsurfing on Day 3

Morning: Early in the morning, set sail around Barcelona's shoreline. To explore the clear seas and take in the city's skyline from a different angle, hire a sailboat or go on a trip. A variety of sailing alternatives are available from businesses like BarcelonaSail and Catamaran Barcelona to suit various tastes.

Barcelona sail

Contact: Phone: +34 722 40 12 99

Address: Moll de Xaloc, 5, 08005 Barcelona, Spain

Afternoon: If you're an adrenaline addict, try your hand at windsurfing at Garraf, a popular location for the sport. With its regular winds and crystal-clear seas, Garraf, a location just outside the city, provides great windsurfing conditions. Learn to windsurf at a facility like Club Nàutic Garraf and feel the rush of gliding over the waves.

Garraf

Club Nàutic Garraf
Contact: Phone: +34 683 60 46 36
Address: Escullera de Ponent, s/n, 08871 Garraf, Barcelona, Spain
Evening: Unwind at the seaside bar and restaurant El Chiringuito de Bogatell, which is renowned for its chill vibe and delectable drinks. Enjoy a cool beverage while seeing the Mediterranean Sea's sunset.

El Chiringuito de Bogatell

El Chiringuito de Bogatell
Contact: Phone: +34 669 01 34 74
Address: Platja del Bogatell, S/N, 08038 Barcelona, Spain
Stand-Up Paddleboarding and Kayaking on Day 4
Morning: Just a short drive from Barcelona, begin your day with a kayaking excursion along the breathtaking Costa Brava. As you paddle around this magnificent

coastline, discover secluded coves, imposing cliffs, and turquoise seas. Companies that provide guided trips and equipment rental include Kayak Costa Brava and Kayak Barcelona.

Costa Brava

Afternoon: Try stand-up paddleboarding (SUP) on the calm Barceloneta Beach seas in the afternoon. With SUP, you may enjoy the ocean while enhancing your core strength and balance. A fun-filled day on the water may be had by renting a paddleboard from one of the numerous rental businesses that line the beach.

Evening: Visit Xiringuito Escribà, a paella-famous beachside restaurant, to celebrate your last evening in Barcelona. Enjoy this classic Spanish cuisine while admiring the breathtaking Mediterranean Sea vistas.

Xiringuito Escribà

Xiringuito Escribà
Contact: Phone: +34 932 21 07 29
Address: Av. del Litoral, 62, 08005 Barcelona, Spain
Departing on day 5
Morning: soak one more leisurely walk down the shore to soak in the stunning coastal views before saying goodbye to Barcelona. Visit the Olympic Port, a bustling port with a variety of eateries, bars, and stores, if time allows.

Olympic Port

Olympic Port
Contact: Phone: +34 933 56 10 16
Address: Passeig Marítim del Port Olímpic, 08005 Barcelona, Spain
Afternoon: Check out of your lodging and go to Barcelona's El Prat Airport to catch your flight. Pack your

treasured mementoes from your Barcelona water sports and leisure vacation.

Practical Travel Tips Needed for a Successful Trip to Barcelona

Barcelona is a fantastic travel location with much to do. It may sometimes be a little difficult to choose what is finest for you given how broad it is.

Here is a compilation of the top Barcelona travel advice and insider tricks to make the most of your trip and experience all Barcelona has to offer.

1. Go during the off-peak season to avoid crowds.

- Barcelona enjoys beautiful weather all year round, although the shoulder seasons of April to July and September to November are particularly tranquil times to visit.
- These months are made even more thrilling by the many festivals and activities that take place throughout them.

2. Purchase advance tickets for attractions.

- Barcelona is a highly popular travel destination, thus it takes little time for tickets to key sites to sell out.
- To ensure that you don't miss out on them, get your tickets in early to take advantage of fantastic offers and discounts.

3. Make the most of the Barcelona metro system.

- Barcelona's metro system, which has over 160 stations and a well-connected network of 12 lines, is a practical method to navigate the city.

- Using the subway will save you money and keep you out of the traffic.

4. Bring sunglasses, hats, and sunscreen.
- Barcelona has year-round sunshine.
- Use lots of sunscreen, suitable sunglasses, and sunhats to protect your skin so you can easily enjoy the city.

5. On the first Sunday, museums are free to enter.
- Many institutions, including the Picasso Museum and the Natural History Museum, forgo their admission prices on the first Sunday of the month.
- Take advantage of this fantastic chance to learn about the history and culture of Spain and Catalonia if you happen to be in the city during this period.

6. Shop at flea markets for souvenirs.
- Visit flea markets to locate lovely trinkets you may buy to bring home for a fair price.
- Particularly, the Els Encants Vells flea market offers affordable rates on silverware, jewellery, paintings, and other items.

7. Tickets for the skip the queue are your best buddies.
- Your time spent visiting Barcelona will be greatly reduced if you purchase skip queue tickets.
- To get amazing bargains and discounts on these tickets and to avoid wasting time in lines, get them online.
- Utilise your time to explore Barcelona as much as you can.

8. Always put on relaxed shoes.
- Barcelona has several sights that are close to one another, so walking is the ideal way to see them all.
- Bring some durable, comfy shoes so you can enjoy Barcelona the most!

9. Be wary of pickpockets.

- With so many visitors, there are also so many frauds. Avoid anybody who approaches you on the street and asks whether you speak English or offers you bracelets or flowers.
- Be on the lookout for pickpockets in crowded locations like flea markets and other busy streets.

10. Discover unusual locations

- Barcelona is home to several well-known tourist destinations, like the Sagrada Familia and Park Guell, yet they are sometimes overcrowded. By travelling to off-the-beaten-path locations, you can experience Barcelona.
- Visit Sant Pau, the Bunkers of Carmel, Santa Maria del Pi, and more places for a distinctive Barcelona experience!

11. Learn some fundamental Catalan manners.

- Although Spanish is commonly spoken in Barcelona and Catalonia is technically a part of Spain, the inhabitants prefer Catalan. Additionally, people often greet one another in this language.
- As you go across Barcelona, learning a few basic Catalan words like bon dia (hello), merci (thank you), and adéu (goodbye) would be quite helpful.

Language and Communication in Barcelona

In Barcelona, Spanish and Catalan are the two main languages spoken. Most locals are bilingual, but knowing some basic phrases in both languages can be helpful. English is also widely understood, especially in tourist areas. It's a good idea to have a translation app handy for any specific needs.

Language and communication in Barcelona reflect the city's rich cultural and linguistic diversity.

Here's a deeper look:

1. Bilingual Environment: Barcelona is situated in Catalonia, a region with a strong cultural identity and its language, Catalan. Both Catalan and Spanish (Castilian) are the official languages in the region. Most locals are fluent in both languages, often using Catalan for daily interactions and Spanish for more formal or business-related communication.

2. Catalan Identity: Catalan is more than just a language; it's an essential part of the region's identity. You'll see signs, menus, and official documents primarily in Catalan. Locals appreciate when visitors attempt to use basic Catalan phrases, as it shows respect for their culture.

3. Code-Switching: Many locals seamlessly switch between Catalan and Spanish based on the context or the person they're speaking with. It's common to start a conversation in Catalan and switch to Spanish if they notice you're more comfortable with it.

4. English Proficiency: English is widely spoken in Barcelona, especially in areas heavily frequented by tourists. People in the hospitality and service industry usually have a good command of English. However, outside of tourist hotspots, English proficiency might vary.

5. Non-Verbal Communication: Non-verbal cues like gestures, facial expressions, and body language play a significant role in communication. Maintaining eye contact, using hand gestures, and smiling can help convey your message effectively, even if you're not fluent in the local languages.

6. Respect for Languages: Showing respect for both Catalan and Spanish languages is appreciated. When addressing someone, starting with a simple "Hola" (hello) and asking if they speak English or Spanish ("¿Hablas inglés/español?") can help set a comfortable tone.

7. Language Apps: Having a translation app on your phone can be a lifesaver. You can easily translate signs, menus, or directions on the go. Just ensure you have the necessary data or a Wi-Fi connection.

8. Language Barrier Solutions: If you encounter a language barrier, don't be discouraged. Many locals are patient and understanding. Simple phrases, pointing, and using visual aids can bridge gaps in communication.

In summary, embracing the linguistic diversity of Barcelona adds depth to your travel experience. While English is commonly spoken, making an effort to use even a few Catalan or Spanish phrases shows respect for the local culture and helps you connect more authentically with the people and the city.

In Barcelona, you'll find a unique linguistic landscape with both Spanish and Catalan being essential for effective communication.

Here are some common phrases in both languages that can be quite helpful for travellers:
Spanish:
Hello - Hola
Goodbye - Adiós
Please - Por favour
Thank you - Gracias

Excuse me / Sorry - Perdón / Disculpa
Yes - Sí
No - No
How much is this? - ¿Cuánto cuesta esto?
Where is...? - ¿Dónde está...?
I would like... - Me gustaría...
Can you help me? - ¿Puede ayudarme?
I don't understand - No entiendo
Water - Agua
Food - Comida
Bathroom - Baño
Catalan:
Hello - Hola
Goodbye - Adéu
Please - Si us plau
Thank you - Gràcies
Excuse me / Sorry - Pardó / Ho sento
Yes - Sí
No - No
How much is this? - Quant val això?
Where is...? - On és...?
I would like... - M'agradaria...
Can you help me? - Em podeu ajudar?
I don't understand - No sentence
Water - Aigua
Food - Menjar
Bathroom - Lavabo

Remember, locals appreciate when travellers make an effort to speak their language, even if it's just a few words. While many people in Barcelona do speak English, using Spanish or Catalan phrases can enhance your experience and make interactions more enjoyable.

Farewell to Barcelona

Saying farewell to Barcelona can be bittersweet, as the city offers a rich tapestry of culture, architecture, and experiences for travellers and tourists. Here's a detailed guide to bidding adieu to this beautiful destination:

Capture Last-Minute Memories:
Before you leave, take a moment to capture some final photos of the iconic sights. Gaudi's architectural marvels like Sagrada Familia and Park Güell, the bustling La Rambla street, and the picturesque beaches provide excellent photo opportunities.

Enjoy a Final Catalan Feast:
Indulge in a memorable meal featuring Catalan cuisine. Savour tapas, paella, and local seafood dishes at a traditional restaurant. Don't forget to pair your meal with some local wines or a refreshing sangria.

Stroll Through the Gothic Quarter:
Take a stroll through the enchanting Gothic Quarter. The narrow alleys, medieval buildings, and charming plazas create an ambience that encapsulates Barcelona's rich history.

Visit a Local Market:
Pay a visit to Mercat de la Boqueria, the famous food market off La Rambla. Sample fresh fruits, local cheeses, cured meats, and other delightful treats that reflect the city's culinary diversity.

Sunset by the Beach:
Head to Barccloneta Beach to witness a stunning sunset over the Mediterranean Sea. Feel the sand beneath your

feet and relish the calming waves as you bid farewell to the beach vibes.

Savor Barcelona's Art Scene:

If you're an art enthusiast, visit Museu Picasso or MACBA (Museum of Contemporary Art Barcelona) to appreciate the city's artistic heritage. These institutions house a remarkable collection of works from different periods.

Collect Souvenirs:

Purchase unique souvenirs like Catalan ceramics, traditional Spanish fans, or locally crafted items to commemorate your time in Barcelona.

Engage in Local Festivities:

Depending on the time of year, there might be local festivals or events taking place. Participate in festivities, parades, or cultural celebrations to experience the local spirit.

Write in Your Travel Journal:

Find a peaceful spot, perhaps a park or a quiet café, and jot down your favourite memories, experiences, and reflections about your time in Barcelona. It's a wonderful way to capture your emotions and thoughts.

Express Gratitude:

Thank the locals you've interacted with during your stay. Whether it's the hotel staff, tour guides, or the friendly people you met along the way, expressing your gratitude is a thoughtful way to end your trip.

Plan Your Return:

As you bid farewell, remind yourself that this goodbye is not forever. Barcelona will always be there, waiting to welcome you back. Start thinking about when you can return to relive the magic.

Stay Present:

Lastly, while saying goodbye can be emotional, make sure to stay present in the moment. Immerse yourself in the sights, sounds, and sensations of the city one last time before you depart.

Remember, farewells are never easy, but they mark the end of one adventure and the beginning of many more to come. Barcelona will forever hold a place in your heart as a city that captivated your senses and left you with cherished memories.

Safe travels!

Printed in Great Britain
by Amazon

46700989R00096